# Mystery Puzzle, Activating Community Voices

## Bernie Weigand

# Table of Contents
### STORY TITLES IN PRINT ~ *Image titles in script*



**TO ORDER** this book,
or any other in the *Images Speak, Words Create* series,

email info@MadroneArtwork.com
or write to 3791 Hilsinger Road, Phoenix, Oregon 97535

To commission new work, or to order any of the images from this
volume in another proportional format, like cards, prints (giclee,
mounted, posterboard), mural, t-shirt, etc., contact the artist at
www.MadroneArtwork.com

# IT BEGINS

I had asked my friend Marti how and what I should share in a talk I would be giving to friends about my work in Tepic, Nayarit, Mexico. She said, "Just share what's in your heart." So I made a list of ten topics and jotted notes underneath them. The ten topics became one painting with ten canvases; the canvases became an activation of others' voices; the activation became a book. I don't remember how. "Mystery" became the theme, perhaps because creative process is too mysterious for mere memory or linear thought. Our own hearts are a mystery to us at times.

Each topic could have become a book. I invite you to fill the white open spaces in my story with yours and others' stories, because this activation is an invitation to connect.

# FINDING AND CONNECTING THE CORE IDEA

I grouped, then taped ten blank, 5"x 7" canvases to the dining room table and painted the background rays across them all. While in that process, I somehow "got" the core idea. When dry, I lettered the core idea on top of the foundation rays, across all of the canvases. When that dried, I lettered the 10 topics, one per canvas, to fit the overall design. I ran embellishments across the individual canvases and into the foundation idea.

The following ten even-numbered pages are images of the ten individual canvases.  The ten images are repeated on pages 28 and 29 for you to cut out and fit together with some friends.

Artists integrate their diverse thoughts with
pieces of their environment
to create and communicate something.
Everyone is creative.

Painting done, now what? I found a piece of tapestry to cut into to matching backs for the canvases. I separated the canvases to glue the tapestry pieces on the backs. It would be a nifty reversible puzzle. I thought. It was a great plan, but I got the tapestry pieces all mixed up: backwards, upside down, and maybe even reversed. I could NOT match the backs together again, and still can't, but that didn't stop the project. At least the backs had a pleasant, finished, tactile texture. See page 24 and the back cover. Good enough. Mistakes can become part of the plan.

The prophetic person perceives
something in the loving heart of God
and from that place
communicates it

I brought the 10 canvases to the talk. While showing them one by one, I shared on each canvas's topic for about a minute, relating it to my project in Tepic. After each segment, I put that canvas in a random arrangement in front of us where all could see.

The canvases then became an activation of *their* voices. I asked those in the group who felt drawn to a particular canvas to pick it up. A musician improvised as they pondered. Then I asked each to share in turn for about a minute what their canvas's concept meant to them. Others commented a bit. Voices and hearts were beautifully heard. We had fun!

Revelation comes from what is True.
Faith ACTS on what Truth reveals.

Once each of their parts were spoken, I asked people to gather around with their pieces and told them that the canvases  were a puzzle for them all to put together.

(On a different day, with a different group, five of us friends did the activation without me sharing anything at all. That afternoon, as each one shared and gave feedback in turn, our theme for the conversation emerged organically and connected us deeply.)

Favor in one's own life,
best used,
honors others.

Then the whole group gathered to engage in the next part: putting the puzzle together. It was interesting to note how they processed, cooperated, and finally got all ten pieces to connect as they were first painted.

Once the canvases come together, and participants see the foundational concept, there is always a collective "Wow!" Even Spanish-speakers without English say "Guau!" (No, dear reader, I will NOT tell you what the pieces look like correctlu assembled!)

"May they be One
as We are One"

People enjoyed expressing their own "voice," hearing the others' thoughts, adding to them and connecting with each other. Many insights and appreciations were gained by all in the oral-aural-kinetic interchange.

While physically piecing the canvases together, participants took diverse roles: all-in children, advisors, administrators, observers, etc. Before I offered my observations of the assembly process, activity and results, I asked the group about *theirs*. It wasn't all about me or my story, but about something MUCH richer and deeper. This leader became a part of the whole group.

Hospitality receives someone's heart
and honors it,
whatever the venue: home, work or
street

# WE EACH SEE IN PART

Putting together
>     our parts and pieces,
>     thoughts and feelings,
>     insights and revelations,
>     our many hands
>     and our very lives
is the essence of community.
We are designed to be together.
My little part is enlarged by everyone else's.
Beautiful!

The amazing beauty in the universe
and our ability to perceive it
are evidence
of our Beautiful Creator

# THINK, SEE, DO – TOGETHER

The process of speaking, listening, then physically working together to find each piece's fit, becomes both visually and conceptually a micro-cosm, an analogy, a parable, of "community" at various levels.  As we live in the awareness of the presence of each other and of God, what do we observe?

As you do this activation,

> OR SOMETHING LIKE IT THAT YOU DESIGN YOURSELVES,
> (adaptation ideas on pages 6, 22 and 26)

you and your group will have your own observations to share. The pre-senter might lead each first to write down observations and thoughts about what the "message" of the activity was. They can then share what they wrote with the whole group or with two to six others. This offers them yet another way to share their voices, to be heard and to connect. Live, instrumental music, while they think and write, can open up ideas.

Transparently sharing authentic lives
is true community.

# CLUES

In several different groups I saw people making the same ASSUMPTIONS during the puzzle assembly. If the assembly process bogs down you can ask leading questions to help folks break free of them, like:

Do the canvases have to be all in the same landscape or portrait orientation?

Do the canvases have to fit exactly corner to corner?

Do the letters have to be all horizontal?

Are you making use of the background colors?

Music, visual art, words, gestures, dance,
all are languages.
To speak to people
in their own heart language honors them.

I've shared these canvases one-on-one and in groups, with English and non-English speakers. Gabi, in Mexico, dealt them out like a deck of cards to her family members gathered around the table. They found the organic theme that wanted to emerge from each of them. Joy, opinions and even the elephant in the room were discussed. It was good that I had let go of "my" pieces and procedures. With control in my friends' hands,  the canvases give shape to conversations about their family matters. I let my work be rearranged by the community. Refreshing!

Your Life Speaks

# Spirit Wind

I KNOW I cut that tapestry for the canvas backsides from one piece of cloth! I may never figure out how the undersides fit together. Some things will never be understood. I often need to instruct my mind that it doesn't have to get stuck trying to fit everything into mental boxes. It can let go. My mind is limited, but my spirit is not. We can observe the effects of the wind, but we cannot see where it started or where it will go. By setting the sails of our attention to work with the wind, we can embrace mysteries: like how two become one, how many parts become one body and how individuals become a community.

Two Friends

You can proceed with the puzzle pieces on pages 28–29, adapt the activation, or make your own pieces. Here is one suggestion for a large group:

### Start

1. On a blank 5" x 7" card, draw one word that represents something very important to you.
2. Try to fill at least half the card with the word.
3. Embellish the word any way you like with colors, lines, etc.
4. Leave some of the background blank for later, when you will join your word to others' words.

### Later

1. Get the word you made and join a table of people who will create a big puzzle combining their words and yours. Chat a lot.
2. Cooperatively arrange each of your words together into an agreed-upon whole.
3. In the arrangement you've chosen, tape the backs of the words to the middle of the table with loops of tape so they won't move as you work together on them. Don't tape them together on top.
4. Begin as a group to fill in the empty backgrounds of the words.
5. Unify the  pieces with lines, colors, images, whatever. Each person should try to add something to each of the others' pieces, so that each one's different styles become part of the whole design. Ask for guidance and permission in adding your part to their parts.
6. As you progress, you can take pictures of yourselves and the work. Text, email, or post the results.
7. Put your pictures and adaptations of this activity online at the "Mystery Puzzle, Activating Community Voices" Facebook page to inspire others.

# Casa Grace
### Tepic, Nayarit, Mexico

To know more about our work in Mexico, which mysteriously initiated this activation puzzle, visit these websites:

www.CasaGrace.org,

where you'll find archives of newsletters, maps, photos, and videos. You can book a stay there as a friend of the Children's home. As a type of private holstel, Casa Grace supports the caregivers at Casa de Niños Frank Gonzáles across the street.

# Service Synergy
### a 501(c)3
### Creating global citizens
### one friendship at a time
www.ServiceSynergy.org

### Casa Grace

is the hospitality arm of Service Synergy.

### Ambassador Service Study

is the educational arm. It's a template curriculum (in progress) for secondary and college students to design individualized service-learning projects abroad, which earn academic credit. A sample learning product is at

www.ambassss.com

An overview is at

https://sites.google.com/site/ambassa-dorstudyservice/

## Mystery Puzzle Kit

Get a complete set of larger, original size, 5"x 7", puzzle pieces on heavy card stock, with assembly instructions and suggestions for play, for $11.11, postage included. Personalize them as you please. $2.50 of each order will go to www.ServiceSynergy.org, our non-profit, educational 501(c)3.

Order from

https://MadroneArtwork.com/images-speak-words-create/

Carefully cut these two pages from the magazine-book.
Then cut out the puzzle pieces to activate your group's voices in your own way.

# Puzzle

# Pieces

Integration
Create

Life on Life

Beauty

Honor
Favor

Hospitality

tiny detail of Fishin Mission Adventure's *Place Face* artwork

What are we creating,
each with our unique expressions?
What do we want to create?

LITHIA PARK
The sound of water in Ashland, Oregon
www.MadroneArtwork.com
vecinos1@msn.com

> ### Lithia Park
>
> a quiet walk reveals
> Ashland's heartbeat:
> mind-washing water music
> dappled with leaf shadows,
> the city's crown.
> A picnic, a book, a friend, a frizbee
> People gather here
> together or alone
> for peace and play
> to shed man's world
> and taste again the Garden

# Place Faces

A **Place Face**, like the one at the left, as a fine art print hung on a wall, starts many conversations about a much-loved place and the people and activities encountered there.

A **Place Face** holds more information and content than a photograph can.

Given or sold to a client, a **Place Face** is the best advertisement: word-of-mouth. Worth a thousand words, each Place Face more than pays for itself.

To see **Place Faces** of homes, businesses, interiors, ranches and tourist attractions see
www.MadroneArtwork.com/place-faces

# Commission Your Vision

I do not see what
the water will become
I am told to pour
into the vessels
but I'll carry it
to the Master of the feast
He'll know what it is
and how to use it

# Why Paint a Book?

Books collect thoughts to share with others in a way that being face-to-face cannot. Books open up the creator to the reader. Though you can put a book down, skim it and skip to the last page, doing thus in a conversation kills it.  Also, you cannot interrupt a writer as you can a speaker. Live conversations organically and naturally  derail, rabbit-trail, and discover themselves. Writing allows a whole thought to emerge without intervention, except for the writer's own process and evolving concept. The art of writing is re-writing, because the very act of putting words down and seeing them creates new perspectives of his idea and gives rise to a better way to express it to the reader, as well as to himself.

Although a reader's life can be  affirmed, confirmed, challenged, even trans-formed by written thoughts, reading is not reciprocal like real-time con-versation. Viewing images is similar: rarely can viewers ask the artist directly what she "means." However, reading-viewing is two-way in a dif-ferent sense: reader-viewers bring their own context to what they read-see. What the reader-viewer already understands within himself is a part of seeing what is outside of himself. In a way, the piece of art or writing looks into the person as he looks into it. One hope's that the work clarifies good things and adds true perspective to what is already in the viewer-reader.

Reading words and viewing images both see thoughts. It is amazing that we can make their thoughts visible. The brain functions for reading and viewing are different, yet the person doing them is one, many-layered individual --mind, soul, emotion, experience, spirit, will, relationships, etc. Multiplied by the reader-viewers' many perspectives, one indi-vidual's creative work gains value as it adds value to the perceiver.

Art and viewing it are visual communication, writing and reading verbal communication. And music? That is another realm of conversation altogether. Humans are blessed to have such a huge range of means to communicate. Let's engage and develop all the means available to know, see, hear, understand and enjoy one another-- and ourselves. Your lives are living letters to those around you. Do enjoy writing and reading them, knowing and being known. Without your ongoing manuscript, other letters are incomplete.

Engage in the conversations.  ~ Bernie

Avenue of the
Boulders
Prospect, Oregon

Bernie Weigand
©7-30-98

# Contributors

This first issue of the series
*Images Speak ~ Words Create,*
*Volume 1, Number 1, Winter 2017,*

## Mystery Puzzle, Activating Community Voices

has only one artist-writer and a few editors and proofers.
Future volumes will be collaborative. All artists will retain copyright.

**Bernie Weigand**, art, writing, editor-in chief
**Jacob Nelson**, editor, InDesign tutor, beloved son (see page 30)
**Joyce Nicholsen**, proof reader, inquirer, and dear friend

# Submissions

# Volume 1, Number 2, Spring 2020

is titled

## Woven Wonders, Tapestries & Backstories

theme: "process"

If you'd like to submit work, or to place an ad in Vol.1, No. 2
inquire at info@MadroneArtwork.com